LITTLE
GIRL BLUE

POEMS

LITTLE GIRL BLUE

POEMS

SEQUOIA MANER
INTRODUCTION BY AMANDA JOHNSTON

Winner of the Fall 2021 Host Publications Chapbook Prize

ISBN: 978-1-7376050-0-3
ISBN short: 1-7376050-0-7

Book Design: Claire Bowman
Cover Design: Annar Veröld

Published by Host Publications, P.O. Box 302920, Austin, TX 78703

www.HostPublications.com

TABLE OF CONTENTS

INTRODUCTION

I met Sequoia Maner January 6, 2015, at a Black Poets Speak Out demonstration in Austin, TX. It was the second public gathering of the BPSO campaign I cofounded with other poets to push back against police brutality and the ongoing killing of Black people by law enforcement and wannabe cops. I remember the weather that day. It was cold. Central Texas was experiencing a severe winter storm and the roads were covered with ice. It was dangerous. We considered postponing the event. After following the weather reports, we decided to continue as planned. The weather would allow a window for us to gather. We did not know who would brave the elements and show up. We just knew we needed to hold space for the people, our people who were tired and angry and desperately needed to scream, cry, and speak out together. We gathered our words, our carefully chosen words from deep in our bodies, and arrived ready for what may come. The venue was packed. The seating filled up quickly and folks stood at the edges and overflowed into the lobby. There, on that powerful and uncertain night, Sequoia had something to say. She stepped forward with an early version of "Black Boy Contrapuntal."

With *Little Girl Blue*, Sequoia continues to take long strides forward in her commitment to poetic excellence and truth telling. Throughout the collection, we are called to witness injustice, to see our dead fully: Trayvon Martin, Sandra Bland, Emmett Till, Natasha McKenna, the victims of the Emanuel AME Church in Charleston, four little girls in Birmingham, and our heroes Harriet Jacobs, Muhammad Ali, Tupac, and Prince. These poems serve in part as the poet's response to a pivotal question from the title poem "Little Girl Blue"—*What you gon' do?* Sequoia shows us she will use the undeniable power of her voice against those who would attempt to destroy us.

As painful as it is to revisit the trauma of such grotesque human realities, Sequoia guides us through our bodies and reminds us we are here to do much more than die. We are here to discover our unique sensual selves through self-discovery and creation. We are here "pruned back to unharmed parts" and reminded of our own names as the poet remembers and claims her own, "Sequoia— / of water & root / of burl & bark / I house life. / I nest families."

Indeed, Sequoia gathers us in these poems as the family we are. We are in this life together and I am thankful for Sequoia's generous poetic heart and scholarly brilliance that crafted this testimony in verse for us to return to again and again so we never forget what has happened and what can be if we dare to show up for ourselves and each other in this thing called life. Now, enter these poems and answer the call. What *you* gon' do?

Amanda Johnston
Round Rock, TX
July 5, 2021

How do we memorialize an event that is still ongoing?

— Christina Sharpe, *In the Wake*

I felt as though I'd been watching a bad comedy. Only it was real and I was living it and it was the only historically meaningful life that I could live.

— Ralph Ellison, *Invisible Man*

LITTLE GIRL BLUE
(A PRELUDE)

Little girl blue, you blewed your horn of
    mourning & warning into whirlwind &
        pollen-squalls. You asked_____where we gon' get
      clean? The lake or the stream? In the break
       or the dream? Or somewhere, someplace,
        in between?

Little girl blue, you traded your horn for cry
    but when you hailed into the gales,
      only a small, faint sigh, & two white doves cooing
      My, oh my

Hey blue girl!   girl blue!

        What you gon' do?

    It's comin.

UPON READING THE AUTOPSY
OF SANDRA BLAND

The words of the medical examiner read "the neck is remarkable for a ligature furrow" / & you are unwoven by the combination of these two words: ligature & furrow / because furrow describes a groove or rut in the ground / or in the surface of something / like tender skin / a furrow is a depression dug out for seeding / how odd the furrowing set next to "ligature" which derives from the Latin *ligare* meaning to tie or bind / the word ligature is tough & flexible / like the larynx / it holds the state of being bound or stiffened / like the body in solitary confinement / like the body in rigor mortis in solitary confinement / it moves beyond the act of binding to capture the thing that performs the act of binding / like a cord / or a similar something / like a plastic bag / but the ligature is also thread used in surgery to close a vessel / or remove a tumor / & you think about how the body is a vessel / & how she had no tumors / how the trachea is an instrument moving currents of air into & out of lungs / how in music a ligature is both the group of notes played as a phrase & the curved line that indicates such a phrase / how remarkable is the spine that is line & curve & holding up all you have ever loved / a single harmonic texture / & you are reminded of how language folds into itself / because the word ligature indicates suspension of intellectual or physical powers / leaves no room for miscarriage or epilepsy or prayer / correspondingly, the ligature refers to a character that combines multiple letters / like the æ in vertebræ / & so many common words once contained space enough for small couplings / words like economy & hemorrhage & tragedy & fetus & federal / & you wonder if Sandra knew that bound up in her furrowing was a history of how easily the body rends.

EPISTLE

But I guarantee that I will spark the brain that changes the world. And that's our job.

— Tupac Shakur, 1994

I.

Dear Tupac,

You are scattered like jazz across these states—
      sorrowful note in Baltimore;
          syncopated bruise in Harlem;
              gravel-mouthed moan in Oakland;
    a mustard seed in Compton.

      You are always already a thefted body—
          torso dislodged from neck & its bullet wounds;
            fingers plucked for preservation;
               skin flayed, stretched for book binding;
         golden tongue gifted to rough waters.

         You are the material evidence of survival
     a lifetime of resurrections
      a discharge of hauntings
      a flashpoint
         the roam & wander of post-bop
   a brilliant star streaking wild across the sky.

You are the ring shout of a radical tradition   a prayer   a self-fulfilling prophecy
          a manifestation of the ecstatic
            the stuff of elegies & uprisings.

        You are the sound a ghost makes when it returns to a body.

II.

Dear Tupac,

Sometimes when I think of you, I gaze at the moon on a clear
night when no wind whips & the coyote slinks through
dampened sage in mountains somewhere far from this city
that is so loud with people & their echoed mournings, so
bright with lights & a steady underlying thrum, where
invisibility is the new black & breath is a chokehold, where
instead of breath, calculations of life after death envisage a
world where no longer does iconicity exhalate the flesh of
boys & a full clip makes right the ritual of second-class
birthings. What a queer art of death this performance of
absence, this ritual of un-making where, for at least a brief
while, the body is witnessed as a body & not a network of
misnamings, not the particulate matter of psychopathy &
urban blight, not a constellation of corporatized desires, not
a symbol of struggle but, simply, a body at odds with an out-
of-control punishment system: can you be black & look at
this?

III.

Dear Tupac, I've enclosed for you a resurrection recipe. May it be useful.

1. Start with three parts legend

2. Peel rib, jaw, and naval

3. Dust with pearlescent opal

3. Mix with the ashes of a bombed-out house in West Philly

4. Find whatever footage you can of Stokely

4. Combine billy club & glock .45

5. Chop funky baseline & the disappointments of integration

6. Grind tattoo into the chalky film of a burning city

7. Blend until viscous

Let rest.
Let rise.

Now, imagine the boy.

Imagine the boy un-bulleted   un-punctured

Imagine the boy intact   unpenetrated

Imagine the boy and his body out of time   not supposed to be   but here, &
breathing, anyway

Imagine the boy not dead.

This is what you've hungered for.

BLACK BOY CONTRAPUNTAL

for Trayvon Martin

I am American **first** impression: I don't belong here anymore

I have black friends & race is **mythic** invisible, odd I am treated like

A civic duty: patrolling the block for **a thug** a nuisance: suspended

Performing the ritual, **again.** A walk to clear the brain.

He stared hard, zeroed in **it rained** drops weighty as bullets.

There's been a history of black boys **breaking** into gated neighborhoods

They always get away **walking** & feeling the need to run

Suspiciously tall; **talking** & feeling the need to yell,

Suspiciously boastful; **tasting** something acrid like adrenaline or

Blood, refusing to call it **fear** concealed in a hoodie

Rising like smoke **visible-invisible** body of a boy

Stand ground. **Move** **steady.** Refuse running.

8

ON THE WALK HOME FROM THE BALLOT BOX, THINKING OF LUCILLE CLIFTON & EVIE SHOCKLEY (NOVEMBER 2016)

ballot
bullet
bottle   *black*   *& blue*
box
bomb
bubble   *black &*   *blue*
bauble
button
baton
border   *oh, what did I do*
broader
bracket
brick
break   *to be*
barracoon   *so*
barrier
bolster
blister
bluster   *black*   *&*   *blue?*
bludgeon
blast off

ON LOSS

you did not think it would feel like this
    being moved from there to here

you have been made into a thing for holding before
    an amulet hung from your lover's neck
    an oar to navigate her heaving waves

unaware of sudden severance
    you feel mis-placed
    from without   unfamiliar

you wonder about your body & its once supple flesh

    you wonder, "what has become of you?"
    dappled thighs spread wide under firm hands
    neck stretched long with insistent kisses

you miss the sensation of possessing a body
    you miss the sensation of you

now that you have been made a thing for moving
    & having been moved from one place
    to another,

from there to here with no warning
no time to prepare for the loss of your body &
its untethering
(because all bodies are tethered to other bodies in space & time)

you have decisions to make

if only you could get past the newness
of your startling thinghood

where the sun doesn't warm like the sun once
warmed your once-body)

(you have no skin)
(you notice it feels colder here

you can no longer measure the curvature of your heart
nor rely on the regularity of its pulsing

you still have memory
you know what ache is

where butterflies fluttered,   only stone.

THE SUBSTANTIA NIGRA OR,
WHAT ALI MIGHT SAY

I crossed water, crossed rights & lefts,
Crossed all borders between myth & man.
I am worthy of all praise, worthy of all praise.

In crossing from Louisville to holy land
I defied the white matter of memory.
I am worthy of all praise, worthy of all praise.

In defiance of nation I blackened blood, opponents,
Butterflies—wherever my hands lay.
I am worthy of all praise, worthy of all praise.

In black-tongued broadcast I forced fortune & fights.
I forced them to call me by my name: Ali.
I am worthy of all praise, worthy of all praise.

"float like a butterfly, sting like a bee"

Emmett gone nearly ten years now & you are reminded how the submerged body will float despite weighting & how those folk were lynched because Jack proved marked men can startle like prismatic color through the static of radio & how those asiatic people in Vietnam might find a vision of Brother Malcolm sparking liberation to be universal truth that men who dare cultivate butterfly philosophies & spread their butterfly wings bear the distinctive hum of the bruised & burning sting nestled deep in tender meat & how a bomb will tear the delicate bodies of four little black girls like a bomb tears the delicate bodies of four little yellow girls too for surely when history pendulates a steady rhythm even the greatest of great nations will sink & plunge in the shadow of the diving bee

***

"impossible is not a declaration, it's a dare"

Emmett gone nearly sixty years now & you are reminded how the broken spine remains the impossible indicator of brokenness despite its breaking & how the spectacle of a splayed & summer-sunned body is nothing more than the symbol re-symbolized & how you've witnessed this before: this record of not conclusive enough to convict this record of not conclusive enough to conclude conclusions this record a watering of grief wetting wings poised for escape & if the thundering be independent declaration called free then wings will regenerate when ceremoniously oiled between bristles that rise along its scarlet underside that is so brittle & so light for under the weight of bulleted blows the body drops like a body drops under the weight of bulleted blows—surely the backward boomerang of history is a dare

***

the butterfly is a veined thing—

pumps blood into wings

moves mass into air,
seeks heat

skirts flame

dances.

TANGLE OF PATHOLOGY

Scan the QR code with your phone or type
HostPublications.com/pages/tangle-of-pathology
into your browser.

FOR NATASHA MCKENNA

who died in Fairfax County, VA, at the hands of tactical officers responsible
for her transfer from jail to a psychiatric facility.

I.

she was sweat & wild wild eyes muttering of rape & how those sometimes
ago are always always happening: the police are following me / the police
are beating me I can't breathe like that boy who covers my mouth then licks
my tears then licks the wound I rub with toothbrush & urine because there
is poison in these walls & the flood is thick thick thick thick

They will just give me psych meds & discharge me.

she was combative irrational nervous aggressive paranoid depressive
growling thrashing spitting naked & strong like a demon, strong like
nothing you've ever seen, strong like two sets of handcuffs & still fighting,
strong like tied down hooded & still fighting, strong like pepper spray ain't
nothin', strong like four CED shocks in two minutes, strong like it took all
of us to put her down: she was extraordinary

My boyfriend told me not to leave jail.

she was hotter than any human can withstand: tears / sweat / shit / piss / bile
& blood, like everything that come out of her was molten lava all over the
sidewalk in front of Home Depot on a Tuesday as ordinary as any other day
when the hot hot sun beats the face & no wind blows, as ordinary as any
other day when traffic backs up the main roads & weariness does what
weariness does, as ordinary as any other day when the police wrestle a
woman down to concrete to be broken in

Am I going to be arrested?

II.

If sometimes my mind gets to wandering from this plane to where sound gives way to silence
If sometimes my tongue talks as other tongues malformed, garbled
If sometimes my clenched fist craves the give & crack of firm flesh, soft organ
If sometimes there is no joy
If sometimes the cries of my babygirl cannot move me
If sometimes her eyes look like mine, almonds, but most times I see him
If sometimes I think she have this thing that comes up out of me
If sometimes the pitch of black is a coppery conduit to brackish waters
If sometimes there is joy
If sometimes there is no joy
If sometimes the sweet smell of sumac sends me spiraling to dream & I wake up yelling again
If sometimes I don't remember how my inside thoughts crawled out of me to land as spit
If sometimes I just need a muthafucka to back up
If sometimes I need the walls to reflect the funkiness of the human condition
If sometimes a wasting cannot be quieted
If sometimes I cannot be quieted
If sometimes it is what I always expected it was

You promised you wouldn't kill me.
I didn't do anything.

HUSH LITTLE BLUE GIRL (INTERLUDE)

Hush little blue girl, don't say nary a thing
You know how to conserve energy for spring

Mama's lived through freeze that chokes bloom
Taught you to build an interior room (just for you)—

      A sovereign space outside of time
         A direct conduit to the sublime
            the unruly & unconfined
                  Designed & divined with only you in mind—(*oh my, oh my*)

Hush little blue girl, learn to distill the sounds
Of a dying empire. Be like fungi: cross-talk below ground

Get good with being muddy—

Embrace soil.

Grow wild.

THE DAY PRINCE DIED

How could you, babe, leave me in the dark?

— Prince, "Dark"

the day Prince died she devolved n2 muteness / returned 2 stubborn silence / sucked her thumb / curled n2 herself / lashed out @ ne1 bold enuff 2 ask how r u? / wander-wondered / danced profusely / returned 2 a time when her name was Desire—pronounced Desireé / when everything was erotic / when everything was beautiful, strange & they were faggots / when she fainted b4 the 4th encore & revived by the finale / when he was ageless & she was agile / they risked it all / leapt w/ abandon / landed in deep plié / full 2nd / graceful as Alvin Ailey dancers n revolution—revelation / she always landed on her feet / let the music b her guide / 2 getting off proper / she fucked girls / she fucked guys / liked fucking herself most / didn't believe in nasty bodies nor sin / knew her body & what 2 do / knew the difference btween feel right & feel wrong / found a creamy center / said i would die 4 u / said nothing compares 2 u / said i wanna be ur lover baby / jacked them off b4 blotting her black lipstick / she married a man / she married a woman / she was always alone / said i don't understand y u have 2 hurt me baby / hurt me in the dark

ON COMING OUT AT SEVENTEEN

"First time I got the full sight of Shug Avery long black body with it black plum
nipples, look like her mouth, I thought I had turned into a man."
— Alice Walker, *The Color Purple*

When on the verge of ripening into plums,
Some girls dream of sunsets & of other girls
Some girls dream of bursting beneath darkening sky
Some girls dream of her body as book while
Tasting the bitter of their own skins
When on the verge of ripening into plums
Plucked to be eaten or preserved
Through gentle pressure & a slight twist,
Some girls dream of bursting beneath darkening sky
Split to open center & amaranthine flesh,
Pruned back to unharmed parts
When on the verge of ripening into plums
In the middle of concrete cities where fruit
Coats pavement & smoke shadows the moon
Some girls dream of bursting beneath darkening sky—
Water her roots; Cut back her branches &
Turn her full-faced to sun
When on the verge of ripening into plums—
Some girls dream of bursting.

HOW I CAME TO REMEMBER
MY NAME

if desire is held in the body
is slippery & of flesh
is memory & murk
then second sight begets second chances
if desire is dream & sensation
then relinquish the body
& call me by my Name
if desire refuses suppression
is always/already regret
then lick salt
from the corners of my mouth
& spit copper into the night
if desire demands pleasure
pluck one thousand strings
soak in a bath of chamomile & lavender
touch me on my inside parts
if desire is possession
& dispossession
then bite your tongue
& bury it
if desire activates the body
pert nipples & taut clit
then shimmer vibrate smell & hum
if desire makes object of subject
then I have forgotten my Name
Sequoia—
of water & root
of burl & bark
I house life.
I nest families.

THE LOOPHOLE OF RETREAT

r
i
s
i
n
g

rising

rising

rising
steamheat heat
steam
steam

steam
smoke

smoke

rising
rising
smoke
smoke
ash soot
soot ash
heatheat
heatheat
rising
heatheat
heatheat
rising
bright
burn
burn
blaze
bright
burnburn
flaming
firefire
firefire
combust
kindling
kindling
kindling
smolder
embers
soot ash
ash soot

LOOPHOLE OF RETREAT

$100 reward will be given for the apprehension and delivery of my Servant Girl HARRIET. She is a light mulatto, 21 years of age, about 5 feet 4 inches high, of a thick and corpulent habit, having on her head a thick covering of black hair that curls naturally, but which can be easily combed ~~straight.~~ She speaks easily and fluently, and has an agreeable carriage and address. Being a good seamstress, she has been accustomed to dress well, has a variety of fine clothes, made in the prevailing fashion, and will probably appear abroad, tricked out in gay and fashionable finery. As this girl absconded from the plantation of my son without any known cause or provocation, it is probable she designs to transport herself to the North. The above reward, with all reasonable charges, will be given for apprehending her, or securing her in any prison or jail with the U. States. All persons are hereby forewarned against harboring or entertaining her, or being in any way instrumental in her escape, under the most rigorous penalties of the law. JAMES NORCOM. Edenton, N.C.

Beloved, I was dreaming of freedom again dreaming of the beginning & end of everything dreaming of the water of life & pure, unadulterated freedom. Light fleecy clouds floating over a dark, troubled sea. Compelled by a mother's instincts & the razor held to my throat, compelled by fiends who bear the shape of men & spring like tigers in stormy, terrific ways, I planned & I planned. I was desperate with woman's pride & deliberate calculation. Knowing the impassable gulf I made a headlong plunge. I resolved to never be conquered.

WHEN BODIES OF WATER EXHALE

"All water has a perfect memory and is forever trying to get back to where it was."

— Toni Morrison

buried bones unbury themselves
sublimate calcium & phosphorous
oceans shift
currents whisper betrayal
when floods drown bodies
under caked mud & dead, dried things
afterbirth a sorrow
a basin of grief
when flood conflates accident & execution
migration & exile
we call this middle passage
when flood overspills the edge of desire
the body leaks wonder
damp brow damp thighs
receded waters
a love beneath
when flood seeds soil
gardens sag heavy with harvest.
Heavy with harvest gardens sag
when flood seeds soil
a love beneath
receded waters
the body leaks wonder
damp brow damp thighs
when flood overspills the edge of desire
we call this middle passage
exile & migration
when flood conflates execution & accident
a basin of grief

afterbirth a sorrow
under caked mud & dead, dried things
when floods drown bodies
currents whisper betrayal
oceans shift
sublimate phosphorous & calcium
buried bones unbury themselves

ON THE OCCASION OF MOVING TO ATLANTA WITH MY LOVER DURING PANDEMIC

Never relocate during a pandemic—
Saharan sand will settle in lungs.

> When the dust settles, we move forward with lungs
> Attuned to the beatitude of breath.

My lover is my breath & we are ten years strong.
We endure the wreck & wretch of sickness.

> The wretchedness of this Time is a sickness—
> Is an organizing principle.

No organization to principles
Can be found. Cattails in late summer bloom.

> I float like the seed of a flower past bloom
> While he studies the ancient art of flight.

We increase transmission during flight,
Touch down as two cranes alighting water.

Our bodies are water; we've waded in waters
Before—we are familiar with movement.

A body is either at rest or moves
With velocity, unless acted against.

At the end of the day, we collapse against
Each other & this feels like a gift.

Beloved, you are my unparalleled gift.
Let us reappear in love. For us, a world.

ON EARTH, SOMETHING IS ALWAYS BURNING

In seaside cities the breeze is steady. The smell of smoke
Carries inland. A neighborhood is burning. A library is burning.
A body burns.

Oh Lord,
The smallest defiance brings a river of fire—On Earth,
Something is always burning.

We find ourselves coughing conversations into ash. We chalk
Charred memories through rubble remains.
We have witnessed so much.

We fold ourselves between wings of crinoline & wax. We dust
Our bodies clean as best we can. We line one deliberate eye
With indigo.

We name ourselves poets.

We call the page something to strain against. We call the poem
A stacking of self & self, *cantus firmus*, however,
The truth is simple.

All of it is propaganda, another way of saying No. Another way
To cleave sense & nonsense. Another way to ask
Unanswerable questions.

How does the moon untether her tides? When might the sky
Cease her burn? Will the boat reach shore or the rocket
Blast us away?

Who are we but the insurgent blue of a blooming flower
On the edge of a barren field?

LITTLE GIRL BLUE (CODA)

Across an ocean of time & sea of space

The current stay swift, the waters rage rage rage!

The cities buckle & the land replenishes—

Proof nothing in this world diminishes

     Your splendor, blue girl;   For energy never dies,

Just moves on   transfigures   makes use

     Revives!

So, go on blue girl, little girl blue!

This world is made of you.

My, oh my.

NOTES

Several poems are informed by and developed from autopsy, police, and other state documents, along with personal testimonies and manifestoes.

"Epistle" borrows a line from Elizabeth Alexander's essay " 'Can you be Black and Look at This? ': Reading the Rodney King Video(s)" and the phrasing of Angela Davis ("out-of-control punishment system").

Latin for "the black substance," the *substantia nigra* is an area of the brain that houses neurons and facilitates movement and speech. Parkinson's disease occurs with the death of dopamine neurons resulting in tremors, imbalance, slurred speech, and slow movement. This poem works through Muhammad Ali's death in 2016 and the cruel paradox of his inability to speak to or about The Movement for Black Lives. "The Substantia Nigra or, What Ali Might Say" contains numerous historical references including Emmett Till, Jack Johnson, Malcolm X, the Vietnam War, the 1963 Birmingham, Alabama, church bombing, and the contemporary murders of Freddie Gray and Mike Brown Jr.

"Tangle of Pathology" is the infamous phrasing of Daniel Patrick Moynihan who, in 1965, argued that black families had been "forced into a matriarchal structure" that is "out of line with the rest of American society" resulting in a community of emasculated men, domineering women, underperforming children, and vicious cycles of poverty (see Moynihan's report, "The Negro Family: The Case for National Action"). Moynihan's conclusion that the non-nuclear structure of families hampered social and economic progress failed to address the depth, breadth, and malevolence of white supremacy at interpersonal and structural levels. My focus on mass shooter Dylann Roof and his family is propelled by Rachel Kaadzi Ghansah's Pulitzer Prize-winning portrait "A Most American Terrorist: The Making of Dylann Roof" (*GQ Magazine*).

"How I Came to Remember My Name" borrows a line from Toni Morrison's seminal 1987 novel *Beloved*.

"When Bodies of Water Exhale" is inspired by Beyoncé's visual album *Lemonade* and accompanies my critical essay "The Ethics of Interiority in the Fiction of Zora Neale Hurston, Alice Walker, and Beyoncé" published in the journal *Meridians: feminism, race, transnationalism*.

"The Loophole of Retreat" is a found poem from Harriet Ann Jacobs's 1861 narrative *Incidents in the Life of a Slave Girl*, written by herself, which recounts how Jacobs escaped her lecherous and cruel slave master, Dr. James Norcom, to ultimately secure freedom for herself and her children by hiding in the garret space ("the loophole of retreat") of her grandmother's house for seven years before fleeing North. This poem is dedicated to my students who have sought fugitivity with me over the years.

"On the Occasion of Moving to Atlanta with My Lover During Pandemic" is, in part, a duplex after Jericho Brown's invented from in his Pulitzer Prize-winning book *The Tradition*.

ACKNOWLEDGMENTS

Thank you to all who have provided feedback, encouraged, and/or facilitated the publication of these poems including, in no particular order:

Denise V. Maner, MD / Amanda Johnston / Helena Woodard / Chad Bennett / Kevin Quashie / Deborah Paredez / Ananias Johnson / drea brown / Evie Shockley / Patricia Smith / Cindy Huyser / Natasha Trethewey / Tara Betts / Emily Ruth Rutter / darlene anita scott / Tina Posner / Roger Reeves / Douglas Kearney / mónica teresa ortiz / Howard Rambsy / Lisa L. Moore / Susan Post and BookWoman / sam sax / Beth Consetta Rubel / Keith Woodard / Travis Helms and the LOGOS Poetry Collective / John Fry / Kelene Blake / Meta DuEwa Jones / Samiya Bashir / Katelin Kelly / Bettina Judd / NEH Summer Institute: Black Poetry after the Black Arts Movement / Nikky Finney / Celeste Guzmán Mendoza

Special thanks to the Host Publications editorial team: Claire Bowman / Annar Veröld / Joe Bratcher III / Austin Rodenbiker

"Upon Reading the Autopsy of Sandra Bland" was a finalist for the 2017 Gwendolyn Brooks Poetry Prize, judged by Patricia Smith, and is published in *Obsidian: Literature & Arts in the African Diaspora* (43.2).

"Black Boy Contrapuntal" was a finalist for *The Feminist Wire*'s first annual Poetry Prize, judged by Evie Shockley, and is published in *The Feminist Wire*.

The abovementioned poems are republished in my co-edited book *Revisiting the Elegy in the Black Lives Matter Era* (Routledge, 2020).

"The Substantia Nigra or, What Ali Might Say" and "When Bodies of Water Exhale" are published in *The Langston Hughes Review*.

"For Natasha McKenna" and "The Loophole of Retreat" are published in *Auburn Avenue*.

"On the Occasion of Moving to Atlanta with My Lover During Pandemic," "Little Girl Blue (a Prelude)," and "Little Girl Blue (Coda)" are published in *Sou'wester*.

THE HOST PUBLICATIONS CHAPBOOK PRIZE

Our chapbook prize embodies our values as a small, community-oriented press by elevating the voices of women writers. The prize awards publication, $1000, 25 copies of the published chapbook, a book launch at Malvern Books, and national distribution with energetic publicity and promotion.

Sequoia Maner is an Assistant Professor of African American Literature at Spelman College. She is a co-editor of the critical-creative book *Revisiting the Elegy in the Black Lives Matter Era* (Routledge, 2020) and at work on a forthcoming book regarding Kendrick Lamar's album *To Pimp a Butterfly* for the 33 1/3 series (Bloomsbury). Her writing has been published in *Auburn Avenue*, *The Feminist Wire*, *Meridians*, *Obsidian*, *The Langston Hughes Review*, and other venues.